TOKYO LOVE
SPRING FEVER 1994

Special Thanks from Nan Goldin

Yasuko Takahashi

Makiko Endo

Christine Fenzl

Shigeo Goto

Keiko Hirayama

Keiko Toyoda

Yoko Sawada

Takashi Homma

Marina Berio

Yasumasa Yonehara

Takaho Inoue

Chiga Ogawa

Hideoki Okanari

Chikashi Kasai

Kǽramel

Shigenobu Umeki

Yurie Nagashima

Kiyohiko Tanaka

Kana Kirishima

David Armstrong

Jenna Ward

Kazuo Miyabe

Izumi Oigo

Pink Soda

Todd's Copy Shop, New York

Yukihiro Kato

Terumi Kawaguchi

Sonoko Nishikawa

Yuko Mizuta

Isao Tsuge

Kyoji Takahashi

Nobuyoshi Araki, Nan Goldin: *Tokyo Love*

Editing: Shigeo Goto
Design: Masayoshi Nakajo
Production: Shiseido (Keiko Hirayama)
Hon-Hon-Do (Ryuichi Sakamoto)
Co-operation: Noriko Fuku
Color Separations: Koho Co., Ltd., Tokyo
Printing: Steidl, Göttingen

Head Office: Weinbergstrasse 22a, CH-8001 Zurich / Switzerland
Phone 41 1 261 0910, fax 41 1 261 9262
Distributed in North America by D.A.P., New York City
Distributed in Europe and Asia by Thames and Hudson, London

First Scalo Edition, 1995
ISBN 1-881616-57-6 (E)
ISBN 3-931141-04-7 (G)

Printed in Germany

NAN GOLDIN

NOBUYOSHI ARAKI

Scalo Zurich – Berlin – New York

I want to capture the joys of life. Not "AIDS" or "cancer" or "suffering" but joy. Closing my eyes to those realities, I want to bubble over with pleasure in these pictures. I know that the minute you let go, death comes creeping up from behind. But I want to have a ball anyway. That's exactly what I thought it would be like to work with Nan Goldin. Not to depict death.

Nan has lost so many of her best friends through AIDS. I wanted her to forget these experiences along with all the other sorrows of life and to take pictures in Tokyo. "I will help you get over the death of your wife," she said to me at the very beginning. That was the love between Nan and me.

In short, we wanted to stand on happier shores. You can make a name for yourself by dealing with sorrow and pain—in life, in photography, in literature. But we wanted to throw this suffering overboard and head for life's joys. *Tokyo Love* was a good opportunity to devote ourselves to joy. I want to do more of this kind of photography. I will no longer have any qualms about including laughing faces and open mouths in my repertoire.

Working with Nan on this book, I started doing something I had barely done before: portraits. Together we did about one hundred teenagers. Nan played the melody and I was the percussion. A phenomenon of our age? In any case it was spring when we took the pictures, and the girls were in the throes of adolescence—their first Tokyo spring. You can't simply expose and dismiss what they think and feel. Naturally they have no inhibitions about wearing intimate jewelry and having themselves tattooed; that, too, is a form of self-expression. Looking at these girls we learn what a face is, what fashion is. That is what I wanted to depict: the nude, and how teenagers say, "Wouldn't it be great to make love." Unlike Nan, I wanted to work on the principle of "nonchalance." Without being selective, I wanted to photograph all of them, indiscriminately, whether beautiful or ugly, well-dressed or not. In this sense I want to dedicate this book to *them* as a homage that announces: you are the stars of the day!

NOBUYOSHI ARAKI

When I first saw Nobuyoshi Araki's photographs, I was astounded to discover a man on the other side of the world who is working from the same obsessions as I am. Both of us have made visual diaries of our lives for decades. I came to Japan in 1992 to meet him and realized I wanted to collaborate with him. In Tokyo I was amazed by the beauty of the faces. For the first time in my life I photographed strangers on the street. I sensed change in the air, things boiling up from underground, people coming out, and women emerging with new attitudes.

I came back to Tokyo in the Spring of 1994 to photograph the new Japanese youth and managed to track down my own tribe. I met kids who were so like my own friends and I were in our late teens. I met young women 20 years old who are tougher than me. I found a household of kids who are living by the same beliefs that I did as a teenager, and who have transcended any definitions of hetero or homosexual. I was deeply touched, I fell in love with face after face.

What started as a documentary project emerged as a journey back into my own adolescence, a rebirth of innocence, a time before my community was plagued by AIDS and decimated by drug addiction, a return to the garden.

NAN GOLDIN

NAN GOLDIN

NOBUYOSHI ARAKI

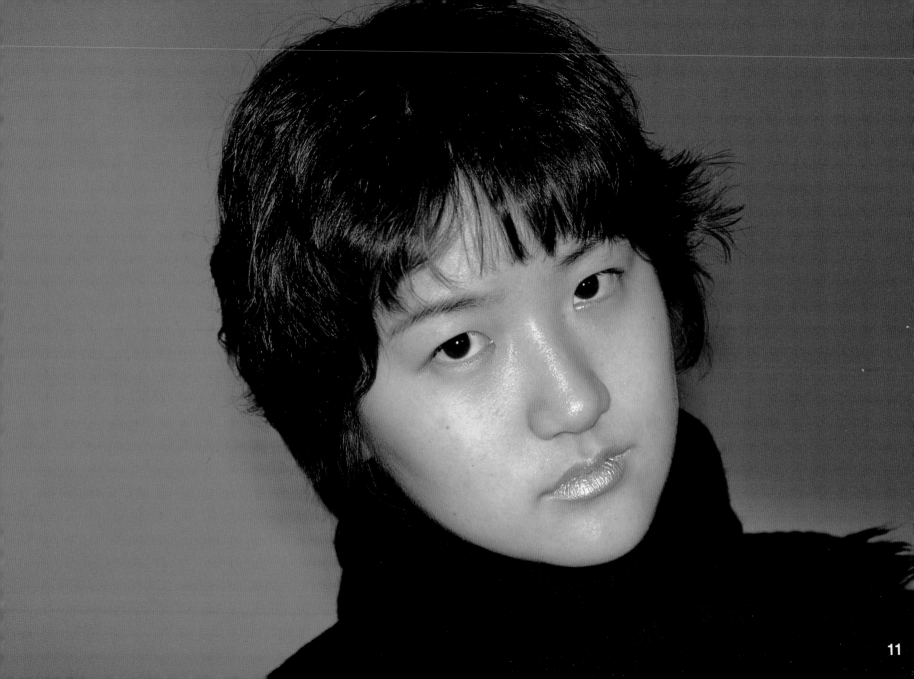

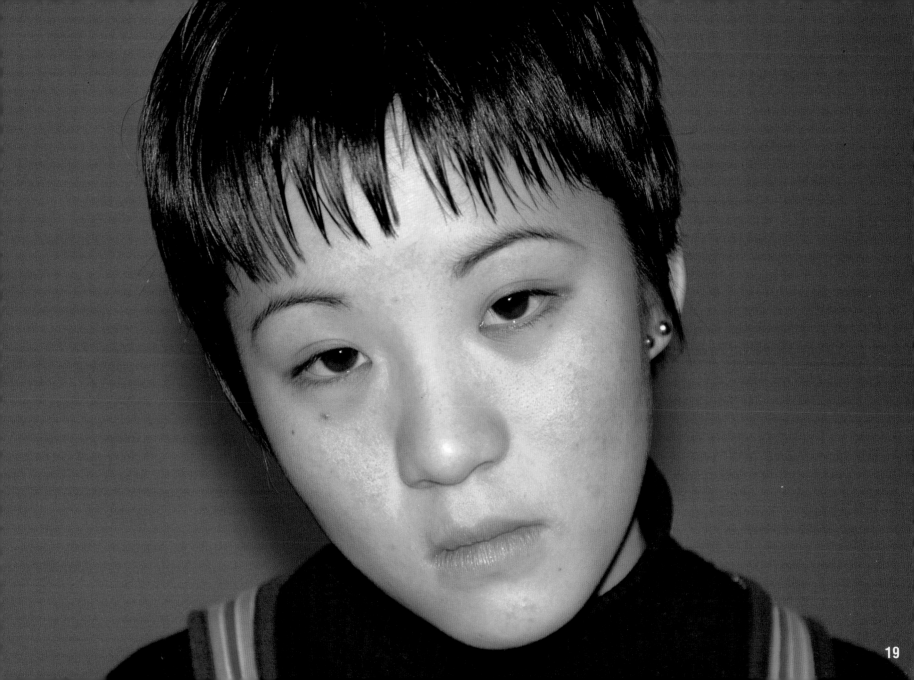

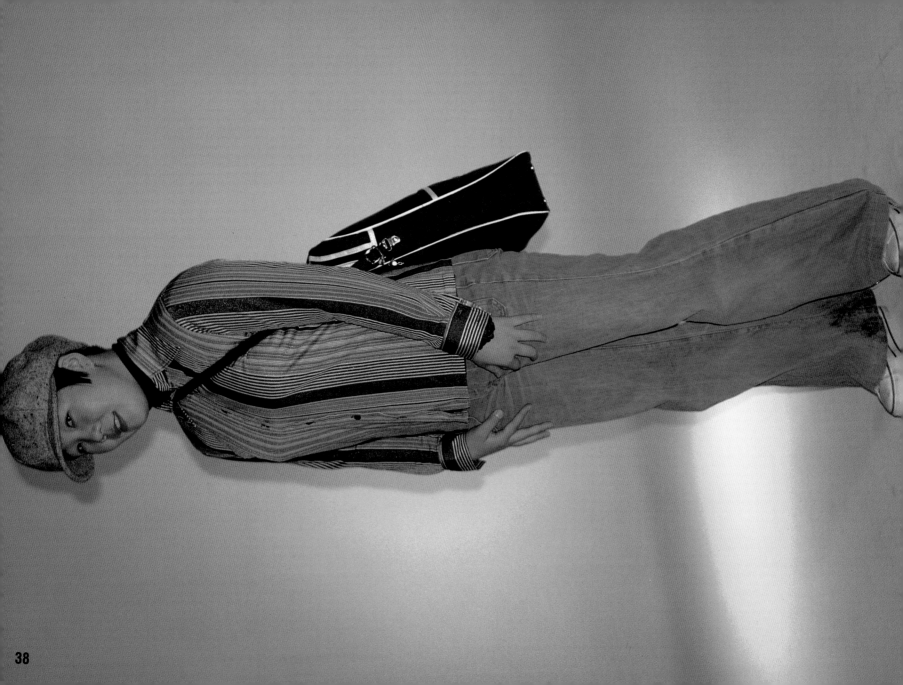

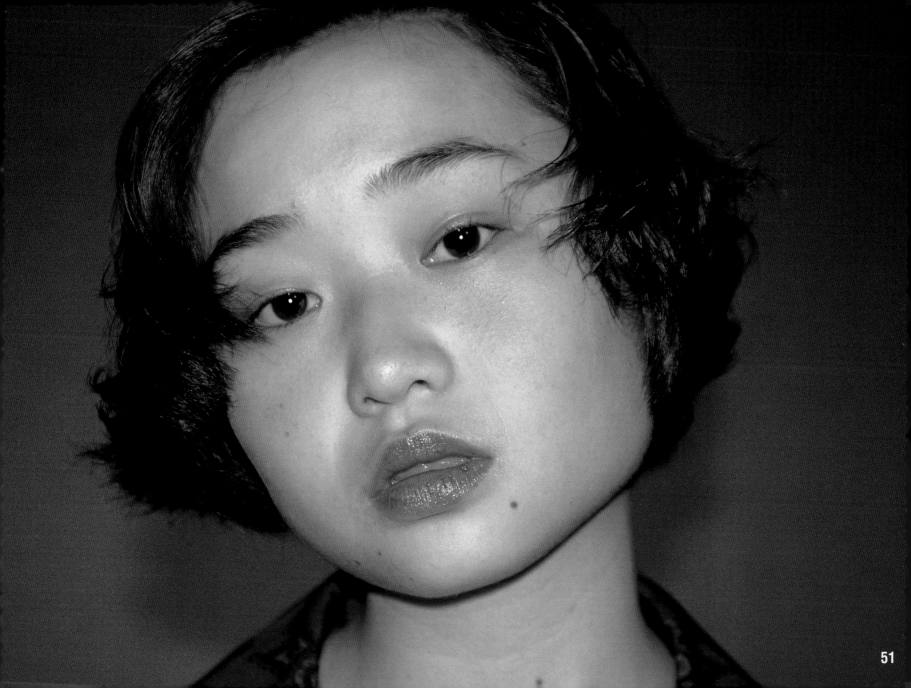

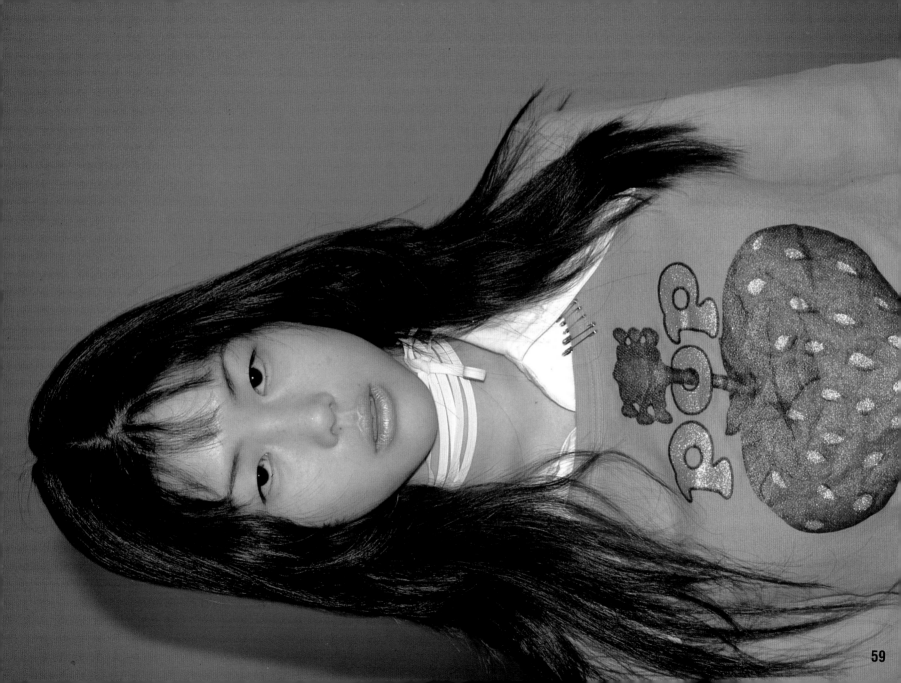

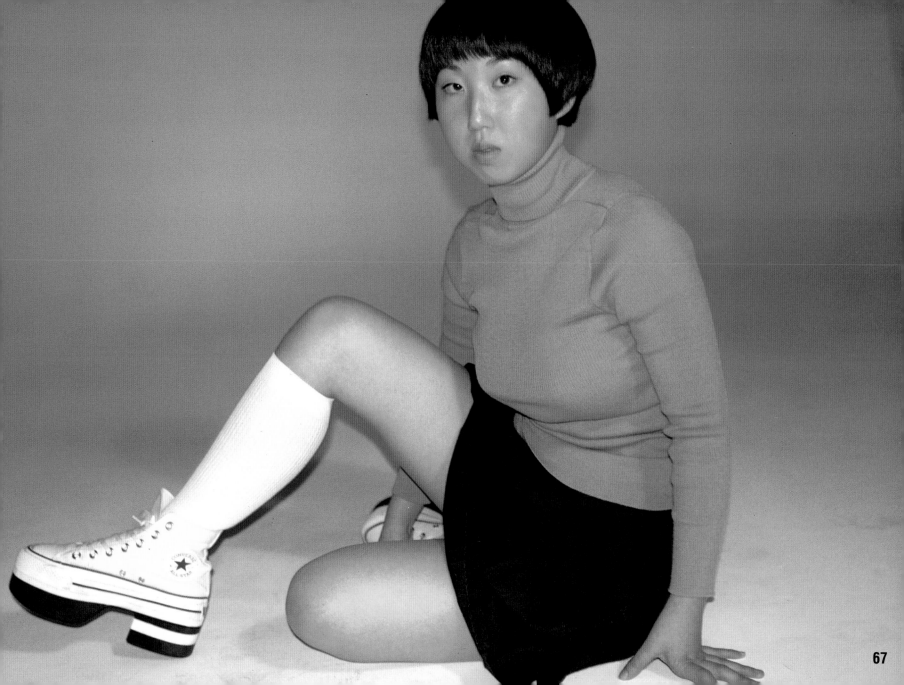

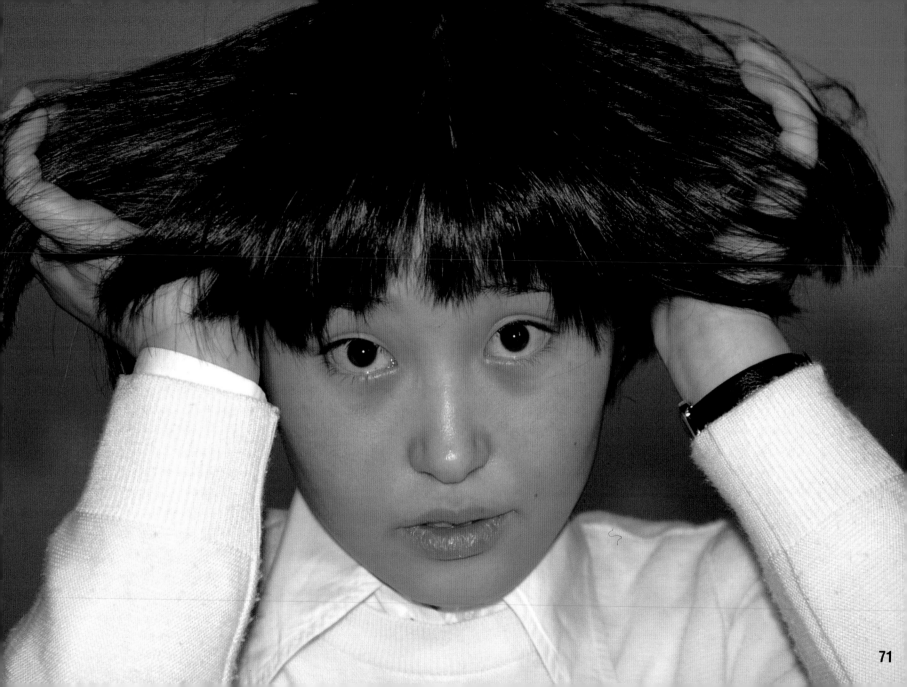

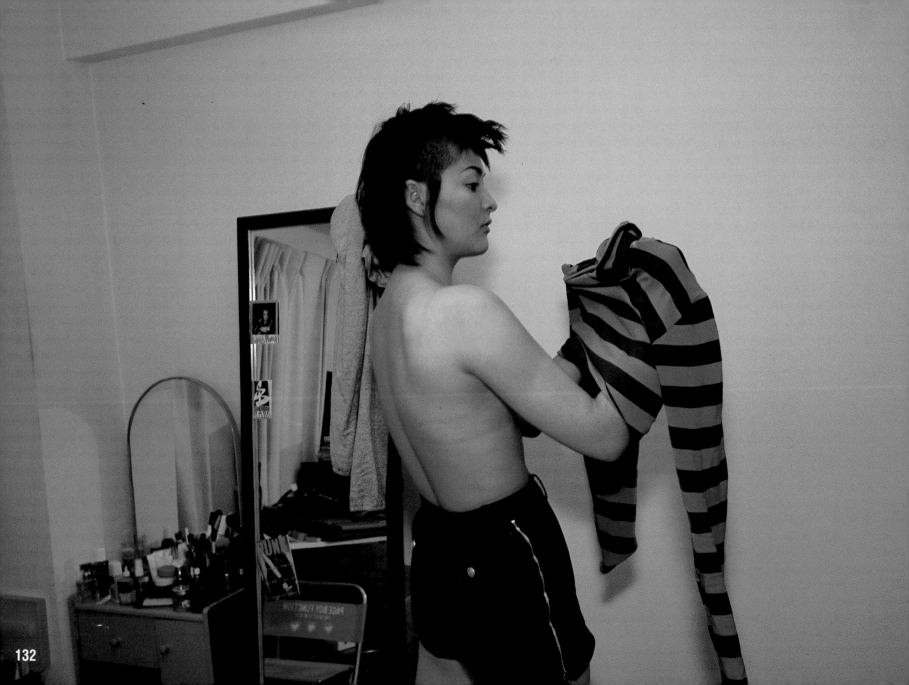

141

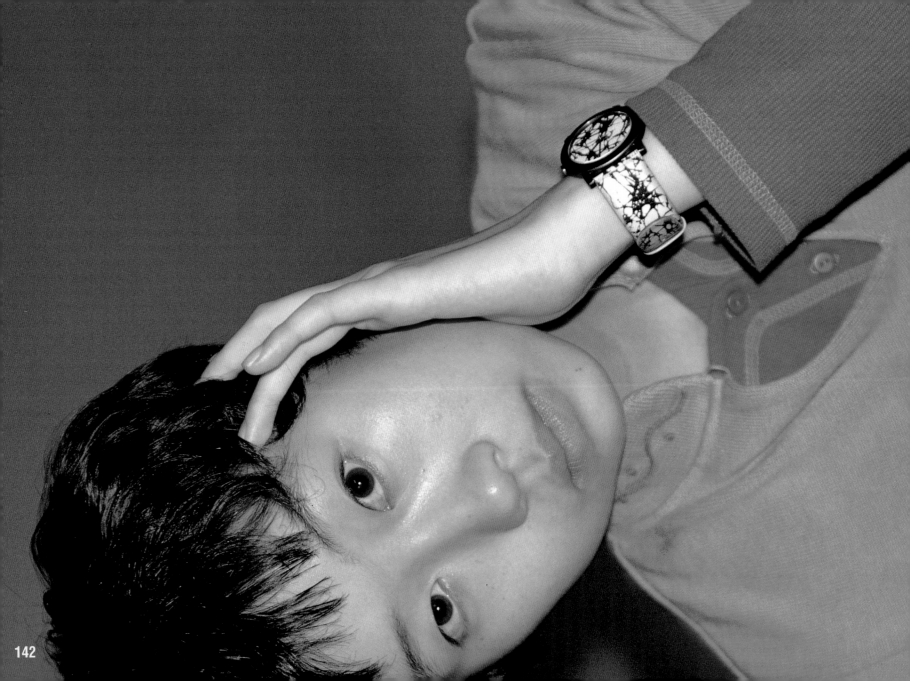

144

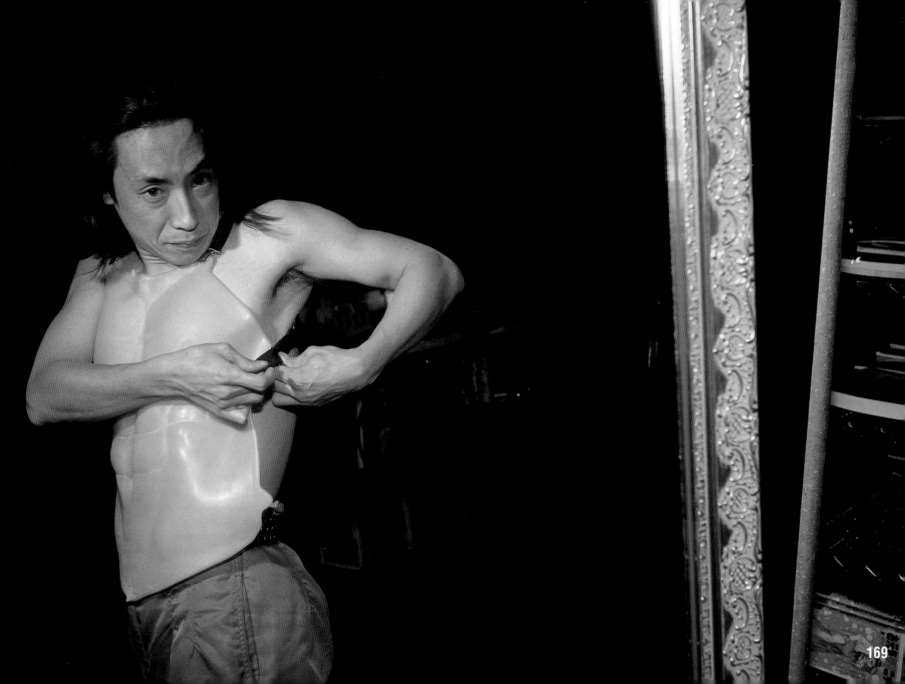

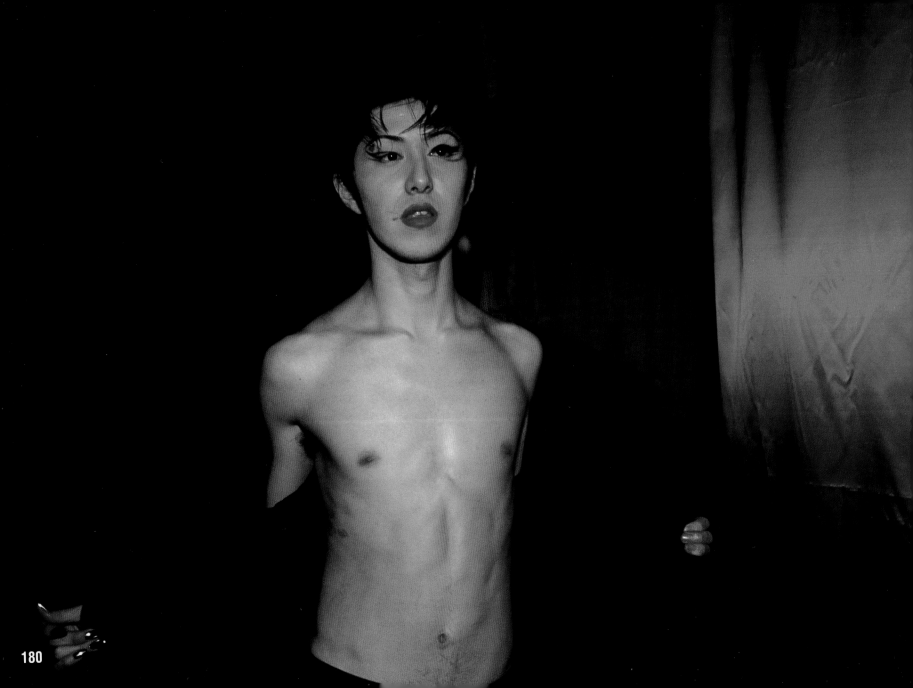

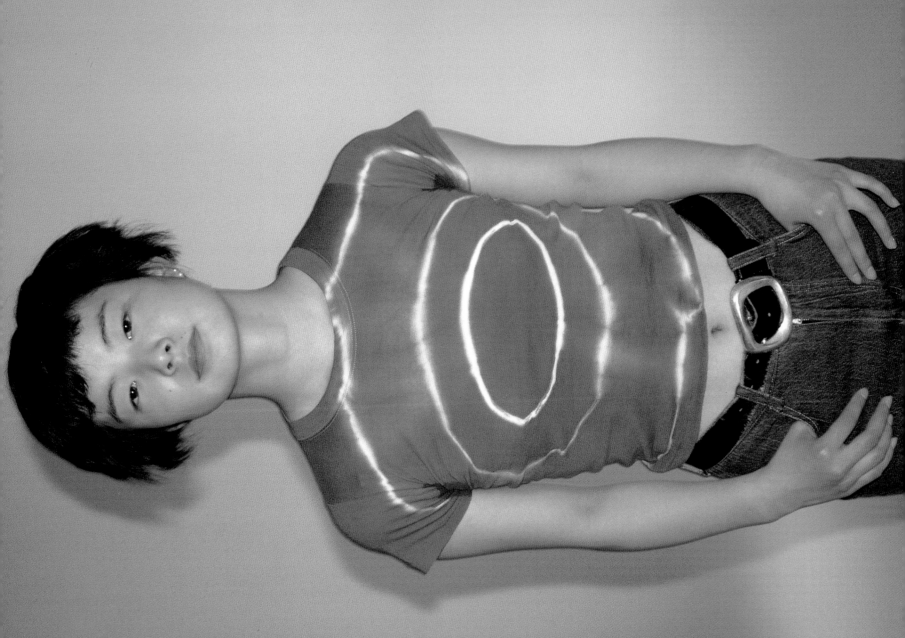

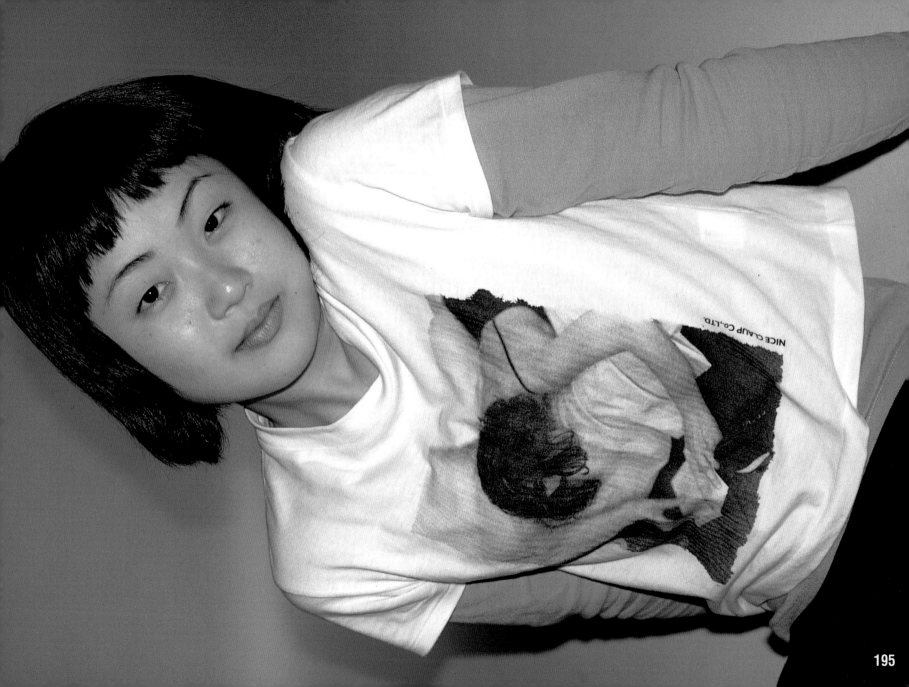

DISCIPLIAN
GYM
15
24th APRIL 1915
(SAT)
at
YELLOW
BUFFET
BANQUET
PASS
CODE V75

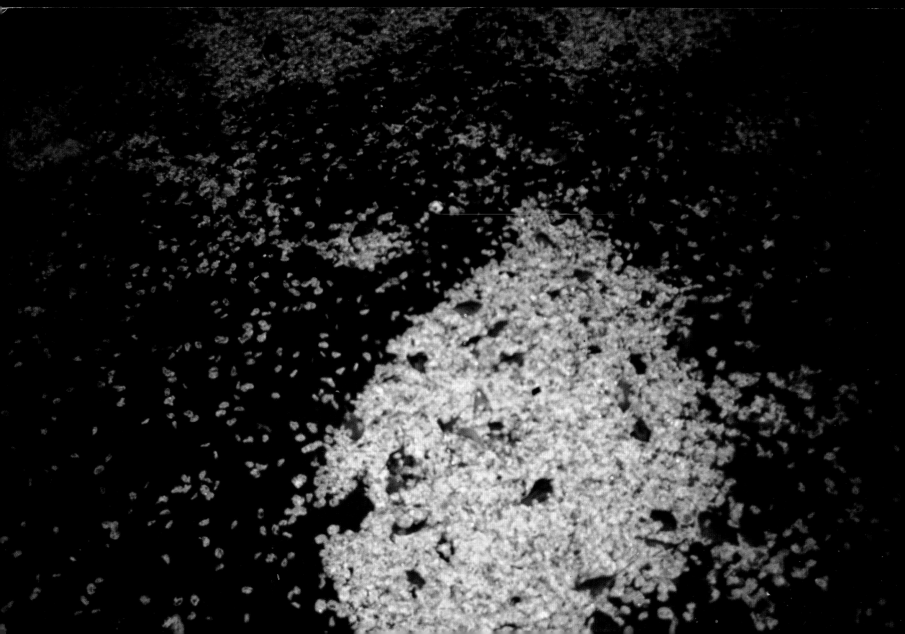